Under This Flesh

Ina Gancheva

For my family and loved ones

For you

For us

Under This Flesh

CONTENTS

1	Cure	35	Jump
2	The Art Within	36	Free
3	Crave	37	To Be
4	Little Too Much	38	Forgive Me
5	Blink	39	Proud
6	Master	40	Deserted Lands
7	Her	41	Your Shape
8	Rain	42	Bigger Things
9	Candle Host	43	My Friend
10	Poison	44	Deep Down
11	The Game	45	Intact
12	Wait	46	The Song
13	Rule	47	Brittle
14	Inner Navigator	48	Your Lover
15	Finale	49	Mirror, Mirror
16	Enough	50	Told
17	Being	51	Robbed
18	Dear	52	Face Quest
19	Hope	53	Fake Time
20	What If	54	Blurry Past
21	Go	55	Loving Invention
22	Now	56	Allow Me
23	Insights	57	Fail
24	Token	58	Blind Spot
25	Layer by Layer	59	The Unknown
26	Ego	60	Loosing Reasons
27	Blame	61	Exchange
28	Staged	62	Sold
29	A Fool	63	A Promise
30	Same Again	64	Thank You
31	Scars	65	Unstuck
32	Shame	66	Antidotes
33	Revenge	67	Hidden Terms
34	Norms	68	Premises

69	Order	93	Tame
70	A Wish	94	Resistance
71	Do Not	95	Priceless
72	Just	96	The Search
73	Higher	97	Seeds
74	Loving Love	98	Beneath
75	Fear	99	If
76	Every Home	100	Wounds
77	At First	101	The Fall
78	Hold	102	Loving Dweller
79	One of Many	103	Commit
80	Stay	104	Bending Powers
81	Noble	105	Opiates
82	Choices	106	Plateau
83	On Pause	107	Ideal
84	Truth	108	Shallow Waters
85	Keep Running	109	A New Place
86	Expectations	110	Labels
87	In Your Name	111	Other Rivers
88	Rapid Cures	112	Profit
89	Noise Release	113	Learning Curve
90	Time	114	Buried Fire
91	Missing	115	Under This Flesh
92	Past Miles		

Foreword

In a world that sometimes feels isolating, each of us carries stories that reflect our unique experiences while also connecting us to the broader human experience. Through my writing, I strive to capture those moments-those instances that, upon reflection, reveal themselves as mirrors of our shared emotions and paths.

From the exhilarating thrill of summer adventures to the quiet chaos of late-night conversations, each poem in this collection seeks to uncover different facets of life that resonate with our deepest selves. I'm particularly drawn to the bittersweet nature of love and friendship-the soaring highs of connection alongside the profound lows of disappointment.

Through play with words, we can bridge the gap between the personal and the universal. And so, I want to dig into the heart of human feelings, exploring both heartbreak and joy to better understand what binds us together. It's a journey into what it truly means to be human-a soulful exploration beneath the surface.

I invite you to join me as we wander through the emotional landscapes that unite us all. Here, every heartbeat echoes with the tales of countless others. Together, we can uncover the beauty found in our shared struggles and triumphs, recognizing that, while our individual experiences may be unique, the emotions they stir are timeless and deeply intertwined.

Yours
IG

Cure

I want to talk about the things we never talk

pretty promises that went into pieces, broke

untold unshared understood wrongly

answers answered way too promptly

I want to talk about the different ways we see

& why these hearts of ours, so often disagree

let one share the lies they tell themselves alone

maybe then the truth at the other can be thrown

let us talk about the ways eyes can only talk

words unjustly decorate the paths they walk

& why not talk about the things that hurt us best

maybe only then we, in the cure, can time invest

I want to talk about all the things we never talk

since loving you weights more than walking off

The Art Within

So, if that piece of art within me leaves

would I turn into a human, but at peace

If one, one day, settles for "normality"

Do they become a part of some banality?

If the art within me began to disappear

would my soul & brain be emptied clear

would I view the world in any different way

and would I become another soul in grey?

The answers one cannot dare to discover

any form of art enhances a plastic cover

A cover that allows me to remain insane

& refuses the world to view me as plain

So, if that piece of art within me goes away

one will most likely stop with words to play

Crave

I am craving everything and all they have

I crave the way they simply share a laugh

My soul wants exactly what they feel

For one another, they would even kill

To need such a thing as theirs is exhausting

Still, having it, I've found to be more costing

Exposure to affection is more or less, a curse

I purposely avoid letting one in crave immerse

Little Too Much

I gave you a little something

a tiny part of my own being

I gave you a little something of myself

and you, you just left it on a dusty shelf

I shared a tiny part of my being, so small

it took me too long, to learn it was my all

Tell me, was it really so hard to keep it safe

I had carried its weight yet, remained sane

Why was it too much to hold it for longer

in contrast to you, it made me stronger

Why was it that, when you kept it away

I turned weak and filled with more pain

Why did you use it to break all that I was

and why did one let it for so long to last

I once gave you a tiny part of my being

was it really so hard to allow it to be it

Blink

I've been thinking recently

Recently I have just been thinking

staring at the ceiling, not blinking

Thinking about this and that

the white wall, I'm staring at

It says nothing to me, me neither in fact

I've just been thinking what if it cracked

What will come out if it opens right now

Will the wall fall on me, if so, then how

Would tiny pieces crash on my face

or would it all ruin the entire place

If so it cracks, how can it be fixed later

would fixing it, mean a danger greater

If so, the wall I'm staring at, falls on me

do I leave now, or wait my falling to see

I'm looking for answers and so I've been thinking a lot

If I put all my trust in this wall, would it still on one fall

Master

It is so pathetic

It almost seems poetic

It revealed your self-conceit so greatly

the unravelling, quiet, almost sedately

the sequel of it was skilfully hidden

it got you too often leaving forgiven

Your love, until now, is my greatest regret

pathetically poisoned me in every aspect

At no time did I regard oneself as an art master

but agony painting, I found a delightful disaster

depicting those feelings was insanely pleasing

the pathetic illusion that got my heart freezing

For that one felt your love as so poetic

little did I know, it was rather pathetic

Her

The sad

The angry

The frustrated her

is by far her most artistic self

So do not mind one whilst she screams

that's her attempt to share lost dreams

and do not mind her bloody tears

illustrating her unconscious fears

and please, do not mind her hating tongue

although, its honesty could leave you stung

Her art wouldn't threaten a vulnerable soul

except those willingly by frames controlled

Those frames may limit them to see her as artistic

her approach may be wrong but in no way sadistic

and you may not totally trust her yet

but she is art hard to ignore or forget

Consider your gut honest when it tells you "She is art"

despite her most artistic self, deriving from places dark

Rain

Are the flowers in your head still growing

Is the blood in your veins freely flowing

Or are they limited by outside means

such as moving figures on flat screens

Do you regularly water those dying flowers

or did you grant control to higher powers?

You foolish being with no own eyes to see

the child in you knew how to swim the sea

Forgotten now, the world around seems rather plain

Let your child in, your flowers don't grow without rain

Candle Host

The desire for holding a candle that shimmers only for me

a candle longing for my true colours over others it can see

It takes a second to light a candle

a misstep & it's too much to handle

The desire to hold your very own light

does not occur with an odds-on ignite

the desire itself is run by an empty need

a need for praise of one's value, a greed

It is a greed indeed as one cannot accept

dignity is not defined by candles' neglect

Of course, candle masters we wish to become

yet no one is ever ready for a tragic outcome

As every time a candle you hold, dies out

a colour of yours you unknowingly doubt

Hence, if you desire a candle longing for you at most

long for your true colours first, then be a candle host

Poison

Without touching a single body part

she somehow can touch your heart

Her so human soul is a true poetry piece

one that can't leave your mind in peace

She challenges every single nerve in you

a different illness she is, not a regular flu

Your life is in danger, when she is around

in her lying tongue you'll certainly drawn

She is a piece of poetry that pleases a reader

induced by poison, he follows the blind leader

and soon finds himself in a sea of fears and sins

where bodies connect only through naked skins

And when that is over, her poetry finds its end

in your naked foolish soul filled with her scent

A fool you are, a fool she unmistakably is

No, her foolish poetry was a lie not a kiss

A lie that will awaken your pretentious self

her poetry is to be felt, not to sell you 'help'

So, when you read her, try to avoid getting lost

No, her poetic lies don't cover 'insurance cost'

The Game

I am envious of them, who fall for me

Believing they'll leave untangled, free

But one has skilfully mastered her game

Knows how to leave cold hearts in flame

Keeping busy, always one step ahead

Doesn't feel, makes them fall instead

You may know, one was hurt so badly

She has a duty- hurting others gladly

She envies all sorts of human beings

Who remind her of once felt feelings

They entertain her & so offer her a lot

But her little stage show is all she's got

Wait

Remember, when you feel lonely

You belong to one, yourself only

And only one can tell you what to do

But can one teach you feelings too?

We have no control over our hearts

Yet, they are capable of loving arts

All we need is learn to our senses match

Hearts to words with effort get attached

Matching those with your very actions

Disappoint the everyday distractions

One day, when your beating heart learns its lesson

You'll be prepared for the long-waited love session

Rule

We are roaming this world alone

Needn't of others as a backbone

Adept enough at loving other souls

Yet on duty to fill in our empty holes

Do not let another fill them in for you

Do not grow seeking in others rescue

Do not forget to put yourself first

Do not be fooled by others' thirst

The rule is plain, you are one and only

Inner growing happens, happens slowly

Inner Navigator

We all possess an inner navigator

One to our every step- decorator

One that leads us to meet the unexpected

& keeps us with our souls well-connected

Every time we prefer to ignore its voice

we find it hard to meet the next choice

as its gravitational powers pull the body back

to pursue the way of meeting needs, not lack

My request of you, is to your inner navigator hear

It knows what to avoid, as well as to what go near

Finale

I dreamt of being an actor, but not in this way

I didn't think applause can be a cause of pain

Yes, you surprised me with your humour

First act, I wish not to be a star, a rumour

The show is over, so just go away

Second act, I do not want to play

I said, I want to entertain the crowd

Finale, not your foolish face of clown

The script is binned, now let me go

Glad to see, you enjoyed the show

Applause to you, using me for your entertainment

I dreamt of being an actor, not your next attainment

Enough

I'm not an idea

Nor am I in fear

So that which you wanted me to become

was gone the moment your loving began

The love for the thing I never was

weak and lost in your hands thus

A fallen bird that is singing no more

your ego fed from a flesh you adore

naked and sore, the way you liked it

never enough, the body- the right fit

In fear one lost precious moments and time

afraid to leave your selfish life and live mine

I am not an idea, and I will never be such

your idea, I fear costed one's life too much

Being

I'm a being, who doesn't want to be

a seeking face that struggles to see

A hole to fill, without pouring in

a place to be, without coming in

A space full of thoughts of a ghost

A living soul, on life pressing pause

For help it is asking but no one can see

one is a being, who does not want to be

Dear

I doubt the moment I am in

I doubt the feelings I do feel

I doubt the things that you did say

Albeit your every word, I still obey

I keep on doubting my own thoughts

eternally unable to connect the dots

I stayed because you asked of thee

to keep up hopes for "you and me"

& when your senses told you "play"

you played my doubts so I can stay

& when I attained the chance to run

doubts again made me stop & turn

yet whilst slowly crawling my way back

the echo of your words, I thought a trap

"Believe me dear, I adore you too!"

Again in doubt, I chose believing you

Hope

And if I ask you the same question now

will truth rest in your answer somehow

Was it love that's genuine or not?

Did you have a second thought?

I beg you to be honest with me

If it was fake, I could break free

Free from hopes for something more

Cease to think of the dreams I store

I might become my own person again

& have the courage to break the chain

Forgive & forget, move on from you

Finally view colours other than blue

So, if I ask you the same question now

Use truthful language if you know how

What If

We are scared of the little things

the invisible, hard to see strings

Eminently terrified of all the "what ifs"

thus push ourselves to edges of cliffs

What kind of fear is this?

One causing us to miss

on the little things full of what we need most

desperately aiming to avoid mistakes or loss

Who are we to distinguish what is best for us

as fear drives us to expect from life the worst

Go

Where do you go when you go to bed?

Do you go back to the happiest moments

or do you reminisce in the past torments?

Do you play a song & get lost in it all night

or do you leave bed to dance to it despite?

Where do you go when your soul gets lost?

Do you begin searching for it, till exhaust?

Or do you let yourself disappear instead

in desperate attempt to finally go to bed

Now

How can I stop to reflect

on the deeply felt neglect

Accused of being "way too needy"

Can we be for loving too greedy?

Adore me now before it's late

we do not know a thing of faith

What we know is less than nothing

Past tears turn to present laughing

Adore me now, before one of us is gone

Postpone love not for tomorrow's dawn

Insights

Learn to love me or simply let me go

study the innate factors of my soul

love me when my character is full of hate

learn to cherish that which I view as fate

one seeks love pure and understanding

scared you may find one too demanding

what I crave is your passion to learn

gain insights of one's desire to burn

learn to love me as unlovable as I can be

attend to one's shared love as if in abbey

Yet if you refuse to pass the course of loving truly

Let me go, so I can focus on the subject I am, fully

Token

When trust is lost, and hearts are broken

words are useless although kindly spoken

When I am here, and you walk other lands

hearts begin to close, and wrap in bands

when your eyes look up and mine down here

seeing different ways to walk becomes a fear

I ache for your touch, your scent, your breath

but I cannot bring affection back from death

& albeit trust is lost, and hearts are broken

loving does not end by looking for a token

Layer by Layer

Showing feelings or just feeling the show

lay back and enjoy it, I will take it all slow

I'll steadily peel off me layer by layer

till I find myself standing utterly bare

Wait, cover your eyes to strengthen your senses

feel a thing and I'll cover all the other expenses

Give me a glimpse of what we could have had

show me that showing feelings is not so bad

Maybe then I will dare to halt the show's ticket box

maybe then I can break the 'showing feelings' locks

Ego

What is eroding me is your egoistic traits

& feeling how much your silence weights

What erodes me is the way you love yourself

to such an extent, you forget to love oneself

What erodes me is when one feels forgotten

& when my heart resembles a thing rotten

Can you for once forget your own needs

& drive your attention to greater deeds

like leaving your ego somewhere far away

so that my soul won't from neglect decay

Because what erodes me most, is your egoistic traits

that cause the place where I adore you close its' gates

Blame

Why let them control your feelings

and give your answers meanings?

They keep you up at night

imagining a flashing light

Restrained, wrapped in your own thoughts

giving you tons of reasons to worry, loads

They blame you for others' mistakes

warning you of "hitting the breaks"

Constantly reminding you that you are alone

making you cautious of leaving the safe zone

You try to mute them & enjoy the sunset

I know the voices poison you with regret

Staged

This tragedy of mine is ironic

An illness that is now chronic

Crying for help yet laughing with tears

A hopeless symphony hidden by cheers

This tragedy of mine has been amusing

The genre of which is now very confusing

Are we right to giggle or should we rather weep

A dramatic end of something staged so cheap

Yes, this tragedy must come to an end

Before I ironically begin on it to depend

A Fool

I am full of love

& a fool for love

I do not recognise this feeling

All I know is the act of healing

So, tell me then if this act I find so aching

Am I a fool to think love is also breaking?

Because I'm a fool for love yet fear it

Like open flame, frantic to go near it

I am full of love to give and share

a cherished thing, a thing so rare

Yet I'd rather stay full & seize this feeling

until the fool in me gets better at healing

Same Again

How do you like me now then?

So different yet the same again

The eyes, the smile, the flesh, all is the same

yet, unlike when they were covered in shame

How do you like me now may I ask?

Without the desired 'needed' mask

The walk, the talk, the motions all is the same

Yet now they don't obey your made-up game

I wish to know how do you like me now

when I at most my ruling tend to allow

The voice, the look, the touch hasn't changed

How do you like the same me, now estranged?

Scars

It was clear, my nudity disgusted you

so did every scar I had ever borne too

inter-wined bones covered by pale skin

and you, gawking at your greatest a sin

undressing covers in attempt to seek nudity

how did you see flesh but not the soul purity?

Now tell me how do I wear this skin back on

when bleeding is to what my scars are prone

And because of how disgusted my being made you feel

The scars I used to treasure, now in anguish try to peel

Shame

Had you no shame, using this body proudly

had I no strength to scream for help loudly?

I must admit, my fault was to need your attention

I did permit you to create my favourite dimension

So here I am now, living in the real world again

lifeless & greedy, well-hidden whenever I feign

Had you no shame, when devouring this soul

Had I no shame giving one when I was whole

I must admit, I have no regrets for what it were

yet if I had shame, I wouldn't have to live in blur

Revenge

I am truly sorry, I feel awful

You've been so thoughtful

And me? Well in misery I used all I built

to make decisions hurtful, causing guilt

Revenge is what for my mistakes I blame

Seeing your faults as cause of my pain

I am truly regretting misusing your trust

& thus, believing in revenge through lust

I am painfully sorry, I am haunted by regret

Now I know, revenge cannot your trust reset

Norms

We are all just ordinary people

undefined like a flower's tepal

Discreetly walking our unknown paths

each of us, focused on their own rafts

Obstructed by ego and selfish conduct

unconsciously by 'moral' norms sucked

Blindly chasing perfection and stability

with the aim of fulfilling a role of utility

We are ordinary people, each a human being

remembering the human in us, is so freeing

Jump

Standing on the edge of this metaphorical cliff

unsure how to move when our legs feel so stiff

Looking below and turning around to go back

Is it late? Have we by now fallen off the track?

Do we dare to jump and forget all that it was

as memories haunt the mind like gravity laws

Can we face the edge without meeting doubt

and have courage to jump without 'opting out'

Together we stand on this metaphorical edge

each of us striving to honour our literal pledge

Free

What do you do when you can't find the answers

with all the questions & question mark dancers

What questions arise when you join the dance

are they so hard to answer at very first glance

Spending eternal time to search for cues

forgetting that in searching, time we lose

Are those answers for us really essential?

When clueless to be could mean potential

for ample events & moments to remember

of which the questions were only an ember

I suggest, next time you get stuck looking for answers

devote time to time, free from question mark dancers

To Be

To be or to be owned

that is the question

To be or to be owned is the perpetual question

Constantly looking for solution or a suggestion

Anything that one can dream of being, is dear

the question I pose is, can you find it right here

We tend to trust that 'better us' will happen later

but doesn't this paint us as our own present traitor

Betraying our dreams for a present dreamer's cause

yet envying them for getting all the earned applause

I am sorry to break it to you, but you are a fool

for wanting to be, yet to being owned giving fuel

Forgive Me

Forgive me please, for being me

Forgive myself for the need to be

Forgive my senses for forsaking you

Forgive me for needing a thing new

Forgive me please, for craving love

Forgive my greed and all the above

I am asking you for forgiveness, nothing more

Forgive me, me, for forgetting myself to adore

Proud

My pride doesn't want you to know

how much of one you used to own

My pride is scared of your hands

your touch & its' insidious plans

You exceeded my pride's expectations

causing many of my life complications

You proved my ego it was wrong

& proudly kept me down for long

But now I'm standing up again

my pride is fine, my ego sane

I thank you, love, for teaching one to feel

My pride's now ready to show its' face real

Deserted Lands

My soul is leaking through my eyes

I got so lost in all those empty cries

The shape of one, today, betrayed

The soul stained, by a nasty shade

Deserted lands my body occupies

with cloudy skies & lack of sunrise

Countless rainy days have passed thus far

with no signs of clear skies or a single star

I cannot say I feel myself again

yet hope lingers within the drain

All I know is that once the rain is over

the sun above me will again takeover

Your Shape

Your shadow has followed me for too long

always behind when I make a step wrong

Your shadow, now covering my own

& mine into a thing daunting grown

Darker, rigid and more difficult to ignore

unrestrained by lights or the closed door

I am afraid my shadow will soon disappear

because my attachment to yours is severe

So, I beg you please, let me go of your shape

before my own shadow attempts an escape

Bigger Things

I don't know how much longer I can do this for

I find myself hating every second from my core

Days pass by but I remain unmoved, static

at unease when it comes to feelings erratic

Sure, the comfort of this secure life is great

but my inner child bigger things does await

I do not know how much longer I can do this for

I never promised my inner child to hatred explore

My Friend

Wherever it is you go

make sure you know

that you carry the sun inside you

& pureness only mastered by few

Keep close to your authentic self, my friend

I would not, in you, anything think to amend

I encourage you to remain yourself without fail

because you carry the sun to wherever you sail

Deep Down

Walking in the middle of the road

my body turns to switch off mode

I walk and hope that someone sees me

yet the thoughts of crashing please me

Whilst manoeuvring occur and lights change

no one seems to find the moving body strange

Physically present yet in mind, a ghost figure

blindly attempting to heart & soul configure

Pull over, I am a ghost who wants you to see me

Deep down, however, I hope a driver un-sees me

Intact

Missing you is my favourite diversion

lavishing time in past-time immersion

How can I replace you with another

when missing you, I would do rather

Do not get me wrong, I do not want you back

I'm not keen on running down the same track

What this longing really means in fact

is that I get to keep my presence intact

Because missing you is not me in despair

but a hobby used to myself attend & repair

The Song

Why is it that the song you've known for years

only now does make sense & brings you tears

Did you grow up

or did you give up

Did you get unfairly hurt

or got to escape the dirt

Are you full of fear now

or keep on asking 'How?'

Do you hope for fairytales

or fancy falling off the rails

Whatever the answer is

this is not another quiz

My advice is: listen to the song

until you learn to dance along

Brittle

Day by day we die a little

our souls becoming brittle

Loosing another piece of feeling

by allowing faulty souls stealing

To avoid any loss, one writes

about dreams & pretty lights

Words are rather easy shared on paper

when no one tries to different shape her

or pronounce her rights as being wrong

& deceptively design attractions strong

Day by day, of the stealing souls be aware

surround yourself with ones that truly care

Your Lover

One kiss and I'm down on my knees

a touch, one's ready for you to seize

I'd let you break every bone in my body

if that meant I would your lover embody

I would believe every single word you say

even when the price for that, I cannot pay

Yet if I get a chance to see you once again

I will cross the road, to walk the other lane

Mirror, Mirror

Mirror, mirror on the wall

who's the fool of them all

Am I one because I try to fix my sins

& celebrate the small or not so wins

Mirror, mirror on the wall please tell me

am I a fool for forbidding them to sell me

but preserve my own being by admitting

that I'm not with social norms well-fitting

To see myself in this unbroken, spotless mirror

by some means helps me view oneself clearer

with hopes for virtuous living with inspiring deeds

mirror on the wall, am I a fool with foolish needs?

Tools

We are humans with beating hearts

filled with hopes, fears & loving arts

These tools of ours, we are unable to control

so, loathe yours not, for minding its' own goal

It could be love, yes, it could also be lust

in its instincts one can learn to fully trust

'the heart wants what it wants' they say

& right they are, your heart, do not betray

Allow it to be it, no matter its chosen form

hearts do much more, than beats perform

Robbed

What did you do to me can I ask

was loving me such a tiring task

Holding my body, yet your hands are empty

You had time to leave me whole, time plenty

Yet, you chose to rob me off my senses

and let me deal with the consequences

As a result, I struggle to kind words hear

and pure from dishonest faces see clear

What did you do, you should've just left

you failed this love, by committing theft

Face Quest

I am so tired of these faces

and settling in empty places

Every face around me seems to have a face

for whom they have devoted time and space

I'm so tired of looking for a face that's new

a face that honours my time & colour blue

Although, every face seems to have one such

surely some are very loving yet deceitful much

So, giving up I am from the face seeking quest

until a face faces me differently from the rest

Fake Time

Fake scenarios playing in my head

with all the things one kept unsaid

These illusions keep me up at night

impeding one's time with daily light

Why do these fake times matter to me

when fake is not what one wants to be

Fake scenarios can exhaust the living soul

Is it truly living if it plays an illusionary role?

Blurry Past

I see a blurry vision of myself & feel dizzy

I see it every day but keep on acting busy

Neglecting the very thing I at most miss

the human I was once is now in dismiss

I miss myself so much, every day & hour

Can I get one back, do I have the power?

Avoidance does not help, I must face the vision

the blurry past is here, running is not a decision

Loving Invention

Exhausted by all the attention

what a 'noble' loving invention

"I will love you forever, if you love me back"

is this our greatest of needs or in trust lack

Unneeded attention is poisoning the youth

detained by seeking in it the real, the truth

All those dying for attention, wrongly think

that loving is a 'give and get', a source link

The 'thinkers' clearly forget, in their detention

there is nothing noble in the love of attention

Allow Me

I didn't ask for your unsolicited advice

nor am I here to agree or compromise

I am here to advocate for my autonomy

not deal with your issues with economy

So, I sit in front of you as human, not a client

asking you for my own sake to be compliant

to listen & allow me to pour my feelings out

without your judgment, accusations, doubt

When I finish, you are free to leave the room

remember to your advice, regularly consume

Fail

My skin and face so pale

I cannot believe, I did fail

I wasn't ready to be used

or get myself this bruised

you had no truthful touch

but eyes which boldly judged

As time went by, I learnt to cover

bruises from each potential lover

In hope I seek a face not judging, real

One day bruises I'll gladly fail to conceal

Blind Spot

A silent discover in despair

detecting lies in each layer

The deeper I go, the more truth I find

deceitful lies to which I've been blind

A silent adventure I have bravely begun

& in despair trying to wrong get undone

How was I not aware of this, my blind spot

How did I get in all the layers of lies caught

No more questions, just my adventure & me

I am ready to face the harsh reality, not flee

In my silent despair I will discover & chase

the truth my blind spot missed to embrace

The Unknown

Absurdly it is to believe in events by chance

yes, coincidences may they seem at glance

but all that happens, is that way for a reason

trying to change it, is to your destiny treason

The unknown, the uncertain may be unnerving

believe it or not, knowing is no more preserving

of your human, honest encounter with living

your chance to endure things often fulfilling

So, trust the unknown, the unnerving, the eerie

Enjoy the uncertain, not a coincidence theory

Losing Reasons

Autumn & Winter, I envy these seasons

they still thrive, despite losing reasons

like fallen leaves, cold nights, empty streets

gracefully allowing new nuances take seats

I envy Autumn & Winter for their composure

in their last days, they don't look for closure

They know to be cold, loose leaves, be raging

but do not become with loss unduly engaging

I am envious of how these seasons lose & build beauty

I wish, I could my fallen leaves see not as cleaning duty

Exchange

I was ready to ruin every single life

& use my will as a sharpened knife

to put my broken pieces back in place

by inflicting pain to each & every face

to laugh at souls who wanted to connect

ironizing them by proudly offering neglect

Mistakenly, I was obsessed with revenge

thinking pain would heal me in exchange

But causing sorrow does not fix broken hearts

planning a revenge is not where healing starts

Sold

Get me out of this body, please

restrained, I call to feel at ease

I do not need this heart in my chest

it keeps inviting the unwanted guest

Get me out of this body torn & shattered

I'd rather have it in green fields scattered

with my heart out of options to assemble

once again, a hopeless love host resemble

I would gladly swap my body, heart & soul

to anyone who prefers a heartfelt loophole

To carry all of this, for me, is not an option

Take it all, hearts are sold in every auction

A Promise

You think you're irreplaceable?

Please, numbers are erasable

I understand, it is hard to believe

even so, are you really that naive

Like it or not, you can be sadly replaced

equally by ones whose love is displaced

Leave the past in the past, simply forget

yes, heartbreaks are not a 'simple' regret

Accept it, there will always be someone better

I promise, you will get the so wanted love letter

One day a loving soul will desire you badly,

teach you trust & how to fall in love madly

A time will come when you won't be replaced

by the one whose love isn't elsewhere placed

Thank You

No milk, no sugar, thank you

a bitter taste is what I'm into

Do not offer me your sweetness

in the search of one's weakness

I regretfully inform you, one's not sweet

my aftertaste isn't of your regular petite

No milk, no sugar, I prefer to taste the bitter

while your lying tongue kept getting sweeter

Unstuck

My favourite song was yours

the lyric kept me long indoors

the melody was stuck in my head

for lasting time after you had fled

To get unstuck, I learnt to hate it first

by playing it on repeat as tears burst

Time passed, the melody began to slowly fade

when I learnt, it was not the song being played

Today, your favourite song is no longer mine

I wish for silence more than melodies benign

Antidotes

Don't we all want to feel protected

from stormy days not get affected

We tend to buy umbrellas & raincoats

for the rainy days, to use as antidotes

Forgetting our purchase when skies are clear

& hoping for protection as a storm gets near

Of course, those objects are simply put 'protection tools'

I wonder, how often we assign their traits to 'human rules'

Hidden Terms

Every letter for the one, once written

reveals secrets behind tongue bitten

Hidden terms, one could not give away

threatened by thoughts of going astray

Those letters, meant for your mailbox

are my effort to begin a noxious detox

Yet, in attempt to write it all with focus on detail

I forgot- my effort always goes to your junk mail

Premises

Refused to enter these premises

due to oaths turned into nemesis

You really should've thought before speaking

What's all this now, consolation prize seeking?

Every promised deed, that was not executed

turned into excuses too often being disputed

Refused to enter today, you choose to play the prey

Knocking on my door won't the price for your lies pay

Order

I am a lost puppet in the crowd

by myself to move, not allowed

Every single step, I am made to make

is there to provide 'them' power intake

If I dare to release myself from this order

I run too high a chance to cause disorder

But if I choose to remain in this circle of power

the puppet show may never reach its last hour

A Wish

I do not want to choose between me

& the person with whom I want to be

How did I get myself in this situation

put up my own being for negotiation

Allowing time to pass is not in my favour

time has come to choose what to savour

my love for being authentic or the love I crave

which one will my sanity preserve, even save

I do not want to be selfish, thus hurt my lover

I only wish not to choose who should recover

Do Not

Do not. Do not shut yourself down

Do not. Do not stop loving me now

Not today, tomorrow or another day

Adore me without any further delay

Do not close your doors to your heart

Do not, from this so real thing, depart

I understand that love might weight you down

But only love will give its hand when you drown

Just

I shall remain your friend, till my heart allows

keep my words to you pure, as if they're vows

I shall remain a friend to you, in every need

forget romantic love & justly see your deed

whatever it is, that you feel confused about

I shall never use 'love' to cause more doubt

I shall remain objective to errors, as a friend you can trust

my heart will accept any mistake, if your love remains just

Higher

Me and you, flying this imaginary plane

a common direction desperate to attain

In our attempts to land in peaceful lands

we failed in committing to holding hands

A distance between the physics we resemble

led our souls to a sense of mutual dissemble

Attempting to fly higher as to see slightly clearer

does not get us, to the senses we look for, nearer

Thus, my suggestion is to land imagination right here

right or wrong, landing anywhere with you I do not fear

Loving Love

The ability to love & give your whole

isn't this the greatest skill of them all

Oh, how I envy humans capable of such skills

embracing risks, uncertain of potential thrills

Ready to give, yet cautious of being taken from

how do I close my umbrella during rain & storm

Some may call it bravery, others- pure insanity

I like to call it 'loving love', a skill it is, not vanity

Fear

I went to this deserted, unknown place

in the hope to get to know my inner face

Now that I am here, meeting this creature

with open heart I'm struggling to reach her

She seems afraid, 'of what?' I frankly ponder

I am here to embrace your needs for wander

Some time went by, but we faced each other at last

I never knew my eyes feared facing all that has passed

Every Home

I seem to be in some ways adapting

to all that keeps my soul distracting

So used to choosing certain paths to roam

certain in every place I reach & call it home

Adapting to the ups and downs seems so right

but bravely making choices isn't always bright

Certain in my destiny, I tend to overlook one fact

every home I adapt to, hides a risk of soul distract

At First

Yes, beginnings are difficult at first

so is being fooled by quick fix thirst

nothing great is gained through an 'easy ride'

even things at first glance easy, cost us pride

The only thing that's certain, is your choosing

this act of freedom often times seems losing

as when we choose one out of two beginnings

we tend to focus on the lost potential winnings

Let's face the facts, every beginning is the end of another such

provided we refuse to give up, the 'happy end' we'll get to touch

Hold

I must admit, I am scared of the future

all that it holds for my wounds & suture

fear of the unknown, creeping from inside

surfacing through smiles, displaying pride

I would like to think, I have it all under control

my inner self, however, seems to lose its' soul

What else is left to do other than restlessly wait

the future holds things for me not open to debate

One of Many

Let us assume that this life is one of many

each one life costs us as much as a penny

Would this make decision making easier for us

& avoiding topics hurtful when open to discuss

If we view this life of many, as another chance

would our forgiving systems be more advance

If this life was cheaper than it is at present time

would paying the price for answers be less prime

Let us assume this life, one of many, will soon end

Do we move on to the next or try to last one amend?

Stay

Tell me when did we become so distant

when did this need of space got instant

steadily the gap keeps on getting larger

no longer the other's 'emotional charger'

I refuse to believe distance caused this mess

hearts stay together despite of place access

So, give me one valid reason for denying our dreams

to me, distancing yourself from love, like fear seems

Noble

There is nothing noble in promising acts

noble should be he who his words backs

throwing words out there, in the open sky

simulating a form of honest exertion imply

There is nothing noble in terms declaration

if those same terms are a false foundation

for illusions that feed from promised deceit

aiming to craft a seemingly noble concrete

Choices

The very feeling I chose to ignore

blinded by one's choice to adore

is the same feeling that evokes regret

in this moment of total & utter neglect

This feeling I chose to ignore back then

haunts my right to choose now & again

This neglect of one's senses whilst falling

led one to question each decision calling

On Pause

We cannot put 'on pause' a romance

shared love is alike to a given chance

so why would we wait for something great

to happen first, before we can, to love relate

There is not a button such as 'pause' on time

take a loving chance now when it's still prime

Do not wait for life events to find their order

shared love is not a chance you can reorder

Truth

I am not responsible for the way you feel

alone we choose how to respond & heal

so do not blame me for your choice to react

to honest terms you so deny to view as fact

I'm not responsible for how you grasp events

only for my own mind's choosing of contents

Do not blame me for the way you choose to feel

I stand responsible behind avoiding truth conceal

Keep Running

Keep away from this, away from that

Keep on running down the lost track

Keep on running until you reach the end

which your racing heart tends to defend

For unknown reasons, running to this place alone

is causing your ambitious soul to turn into a stone

I understand, you want to be a runner, so keep on going

the end, I hope, is what you hope for- a place of knowing

Expectations

Keep your expectations low

or else you may never grow

Expecting too much, costs us means

unaware of what's behind the scenes

Keep your expectations low & you will see

to not expect, is rewarded with a truth key

that opens doors to unexpected potential

for your sanity to bottle the only essential

Accordingly, if you find yourself obsessing with a hope

Ground your expectations & with growing you will cope

In Your Name

If I choose to neglect myself today

turn my back to look the other way

If I so choose to do this thing in your name

wouldn't I place the name of mine in shame

If I allow another, to disregard one in attempt

to feel a high, I then lay open to my contempt

So no, I am not choosing you over my self-respect

I won't turn my back on me to accept your neglect

Rapid Cures

Lately we have been quite impatient

regarding one another as if a patient

everyone around seems to need 'fixing'

rapid cures & solutions keep on mixing

But who is really the one who knows best

aren't we all to the others' destinies guest

What if we were to human flaws more resigned

would that make us to our own fond & not blind

I would like to think that patience will find its way within

the human soul where 'fixing others' is not a prize to win

Noise Release

Only when I can afford the price for silence

will my way clear to my true inner guidance

Only then, will I find in all this chaos, peace

one day when I can afford my noise release

When the day arrives, I will be ready to immerse

in the loudest sharing of the noises not adverse

Only when I can afford to pay such high a price

will my choices be deprived from thinking twice

Time

It seems I tend to leave things as they are

it may seem, this does not get me too far

but when we rely on time at all times, I think

we tend to go further down the destiny link

So, I am willing to take the risk by remaining calm

allow time to take me away from a life I try to palm

as I am certain that if I leave things the way they are

I will live a life I'm meant to, not dream of such afar

Missing

This was supposed to be a happy moment

there's no thrill, nor joy- the tears' opponent

just a blank state of unsureness, of confusion

a colour palette in the process of dark infusion

This was really supposed to be a buzz, a high

yet, right now, it all feels like a collapsing sigh

as I sit in the nothing, I find myself compelled

to reminisce the moment now I want expelled

This was supposed to be my happiest moment

supposedly one wasn't the missing component

Past Miles

So here I am now, laughing when crying

and with each tear, my laughter buying

What a paradox, what a curse it is to be

a destiny I, in despair, attempting to flee

here I am tearing from within, projecting smiles

finding joy, keeping in neglect in the past miles

An emulsion of the very things that do not match

enemies to another, to me- companions hatched

I can't wait for this to pass & finally cry when crying

the mixing of opposing feelings gets my living dying

Tame

There is no one sitting on the opposite side

on the empty chair, cool winds begin a glide

My eyes fully focused on the soulless chair

as my soul tries to align reasons in despair

for the empty chair, not occupied by the one

whose soul I cannot tame again, once done

All I'm asking from you, is to have you seated here

opposite me, & your opposition I ask you to clear

so I understand the reasons for this ghost like chair

whose resident once got my soul to warm hues wear

Resistance

The fight against your own resistance

a thing that requires much persistence

the urge to grow seems insignificant to this

an inner conflict, very often hard to dismiss

resisting the desire to hold everything in hands

let the desire go, resistance signifies the bands

Yes, fighting your own resistance is often tiring

giving up, frees you from insignificant acquiring

Priceless

Time, for me & you, flows in different ways

for you, time revolves around what it pays

for me- an element of great value yet priceless

taken for granted, results in connection lifeless

Time in your eyes is a commodity, a worthless tool

impatiently using it, you're breaking its' first rule

to respect its impacts on life, thus avoid its neglect

by breaking this rule, you lost a precious life aspect

Now that your time flows in uncommon from mine direction

my time investment in yours, cannot pay for our connection

The Search

I search for a thing that doesn't exist

no sign of its' fragments, yet I persist

The searching goes on & on, for days

with every other hope stuck in a haze

I'm in search for a thing in you, I cannot see

my naked eyes detect a locked soul, not free

locked in attainments, success, a fame glory

the thing I search for, isn't a part of this story

Let me be clear, my attempts are not to alter your goals

I'm only in search for your soul which doesn't play roles

Seeds

It is indeed harder than I thought

surely this is not for what I fought

It is much more difficult than I expected

to carry on the moment, I felt connected

All we are given, is not to be taken for granted

the seeds of which we have ourselves planted

To water the seeds of the fruits we treasure is key

but how, when our plant desires elsewhere to be?

It is indeed harder than I thought, to attend to my bond

with the seed I planted, which of me does not feel fond

Beneath

I began to lose the soil beneath my feet

there's nothing to stand on, no concrete

It's almost as if the path I followed vanished

& with that, hopes for a thing solid banished

into lands unreachable for me at present time

my hopes now situated on a hill I cannot climb

because I began to lose the soil beneath my feet

when you ordered your affection of me to retreat

If

If I was to kill, one a killer will be told

a monstrous being, a soul once sold

If I was to please, one will be told a pleaser

a provocative being who's playing a teaser

If I was to forgive, one will be told a forgiver

blind to faults, a greedy for validation giver

If I then dare to love again, why not label me a lover

irrational I'd rather be told than broken hearts' cover

Wounds

We, all of us humans own various of fears

Yet, there's one to which we share tears

one which we cannot judge each other for

yet if you or I admit to it, we're cast 'ignore'

The fear to be rejected, unwanted, a castaway

a fear of feeling your feelings stuck in one-way

We cannot remain indifferent to what we share

so, another's wounds treat as yours- with care

The Fall

This wall that's placed between us

misplaced what we used to call 'us'

The bricks of which we carefully laid

the wrong side of us, cover in shade

We worked to arrange them for support

Remember, we vowed to us never abort?

The bricks of love, care & respect are there

to create a place, we both cherish & share

to lean on it, when feeling doubtful or weak

not to walk around & other bricklayers seek

My whole fondness of you is placed in this wall

misplacing yours, is at present, causing its fall

Loving Dweller

I do not want to be another rumour

a deceitful story, a gossip bloomer

My sorrow is not the next 'best seller'

I'm simply put, another loving dweller

whose leaking soul is waiting for console

from humans who possess hearts-whole

I do not wish to be a rumour, a gripping tale

only the foes would need every grimy detail

If when frail, I seek some comfort on your shoulder

I beg of you, keep not my sorrow in a rumour folder

Commit

I lost the fondness of me once promised

thus, loving terms today seem dishonest

I truly believed, every single touch & look

completely unaware of the turn they took

not to be inserted on another, but instead

cancelled for all & me, never to be spread

as if all you were, was at once sucked inside

the temple of your form, others cannot reside

Promises of fondness, you were not yet ready to commit

but hiding in lonely lands unveils fear you dare not admit

Bending Powers

The minute we attempt to our destiny amend

the powers beyond us, a retribution will send

in some form of bending the truth we believe

as all that occurs is designed to else achieve

Thus, I encourage one to stick to the path given

suppress the itch to discover agents easier driven

to travel down the road that destiny for you has mapped

attempting else, may get one in bending powers trapped

Opiates

Using opiates to forget is not the cure

for dealing with hardships, we endure

Opiates will not solve the issues at hand

they may often call the matter's expand

Thus, creating a vicious circle brought by temptation

where souls turn oblivious to inner wrong motivation

for finding a way, to deal with the things hard to endure

Opiates can't save a soul in search of long-lasting cure

Plateau

I have reached a state of plateau

with no ways of going up or below

a place where silence spreads across

earth in lack of chance for win or loss

Yet, two options appear before my gaze

find comfort here or look for better days

assemble a ladder to climb to higher heights

in hope of getting to a place with rocky sights

Challenge, that is the essence of my inner desire

plateau isn't a place where my soul seeks to retire

Ideal

The kind of loving I look for is immersive

the love in no way, to healing subversive

No, I am not in the search of a love ideal

but I believe that loving is an act surreal

& that is what I am immersed in looking for

an immersion in which, I effortlessly adore

& adored I am back, passionately, profoundly

with no hints of breaking trust formed soundly

the impact of which could be, for a heart, devastating

No, ideal loving I do not pursue, just real, captivating

Shallow Waters

May I just share a word or two

it wasn't all me, it was also you

I wouldn't revolt, had you not cast me in shadow

you wouldn't too, had I not swum in waters shallow

It wasn't all me, nor was it all you, let me say it aloud

neither of us should be standing up, feeling too proud

I would not harm you, had one not felt your coolness

you wouldn't too, had you not found in me cruelness

How about we end this, the way it all once began?

With pure intentions, no notions of a game plan

A New Place

Sometimes the people make the place

thus, it is not the lands we often chase

but the comfort & serenity in human gifts

the very traits, we tend to see in us as ifs

Sometimes the people make the air lighter

in times when air, in our chest, feels tighter

Oftentimes, breathtaking views seem grey

for eyes longtime deprived of humans' ray

thus, it is often not a new place, that we seek

but new people who can, our old ways, tweak

Labels

Can we for once get rid of all the labels

many of which rooted in ancient fables

related to status, ambitions or past acts

personal traits change, they're not facts

I encourage you to stop labels' production

fault & error are part of each life induction

so are the heights, the triumphs, the takings

yet if we were only defined by such makings

we would never get to grow out of any labels

as to root our perception in turning the tables

Other Rivers

I haven't asked of you to run after me

Trace back your steps & you shall see

the way I followed, for you- mostly steeps

my measured pace, you trailed with leaps

I needn't a partner, chasing me from behind

but one alongside me, sharing paths in kind

It is obvious to me, that your direction greatly differs

as the path I am meant to walk, crosses other rivers

Profit

I can no longer afford your company

be the one to your pride accompany

I find it immensely hard to invest in us

when profits come to minus, not plus

as the value of my soul swiftly drops under

the patience line, once the greatest funder

capable of keeping values at a constant height

now fluctuating as your prides my values fight

I can no longer afford to pay for the company of yours

A choice to keep investing, my soul bankruptcy ensures

Learning Curve

When did I become your learning curve

I did not agree to only your needs serve

As far as I remember, the agreement we had

was to love & learn together, for me not a fad

Were we not meant to grow as one, my dear?

Am I mistaken for seeing you now disappear

whilst taking all you've learnt, to foreign scenes

referring your knowledge to "experience means"

I am not an experience, a classroom or a short adventure

nor am I a learning curve, for the unsure ones, to venture

Buried Fires

What is said, flies away, is bygone

what's written remains to count on

for times, when the buried fires emerge

& to suppress them is no longer an urge

We are all well aware of the harmful impact

fires, remember, tend to burn all they attract

Hence, I urge you to note the crucial terms you hear

in this way, from burning again, you can keep clear

Under This Flesh

Under this flesh, lies a radiant spirit

Please come closer, you may hear it

whispers which it whispers, songs it sings

under the flesh, fluttering of broken wings

here lie the truest colours of each creature

the flaws, the pain, every repulsive feature

Here are also the deepest, well-hidden desires

the fondness of others, the care, the white liars

Those properties- interwoven, create an inner mesh

to keep ourselves within the frames, under this flesh